MEGACOSM

Brett Neveu

BROADWAY PLAY PUBLISHING INC
New York
www.broadwayplaypublishing.com
info@broadwayplaypublishing.com

MEGACOSM
© Copyright 2018 Brett Neveu

Cover art by Rich Sparks

First edition: September 2018
I S B N: 978-0-88145-796-4

Book design: Marie Donovan
Page make-up: Adobe InDesign
Typeface: Palatino

MEGACOSM was first produced at A Red Orchid Theatre from 13 January–19 February 2012. The cast and creative contributors were:

BRITT..Danny McCarthy
CHRIS..Lawrence Grimm
SAM...David Steiger
CAROL...Eden Strong

Director..Dado
Stage manager..Christa Van Baale
Assistant stage manager.....................Kelley Anne Keough
Set design...John Dalton
Lighting design..Matt Gawryk
Costume design.......................................Christine Pascual
Sound design..Joseph Court
Props design..Sam Deutsch
Assistant director/Dramaturg.....................Duncan Riddell
Technical director..Walter Briggs
Production danager..Meg Lindsey
Video/Media director...................................Seth Hendricks

CHARACTERS & SETTING

CHRIS, *forties or fifties*
BRITT, *early to mid-thirties*
SAM, *thirties, forties or fifties*
CAROL, *nine or twelve or fourteen*

All characters are gender-neutral

Place: A worn yet brightly painted conference room inside an industrial manufacturing facility.

Time: The near future.

During the original production, the "dolls" were presented as a pre-recorded video using a group of actors dressed in the costumes described within the play. No actual "dolls" were used during the production, given they are meant to be nearly unseen by the naked eye.

We are more ready to try the untried when what we do is inconsequential. Hence the fact that many inventions had their birth as toys.

Eric Hoffer

(*Lights up on a brightly painted corporate conference room. A phone rests on a nearby file cabinet next to a long credenza containing a number of small, closed cabinets.* CHRIS, *wearing semi-casual attire and seated in a tall chair at a long center table, stares at a dictionary-sized brown cardboard box. A few moments pass.* CHRIS *picks up the box and opens it.* CHRIS *looks into the box.* CHRIS's *face slackens, then tightens.* CHRIS *moves a few things around within the box. A long pause.* CHRIS *closes the box and returns it to the table. A few moments pass.*)

(BRITT *enters.* BRITT *wears fashionable corporate garb. Closing the conference room door,* BRITT *smiles brightly at* CHRIS.)

(*A loud explosion roars and flashes in a side window.* CHRIS *hits the floor as* BRITT *somewhat cringes. A few moments pass.* CHRIS *returns to the chair. A pause*)

BRITT: Sorry to keep you waiting. Did anyone ask— (*Beat*) No water or coffee?

CHRIS: No. No thank you.

(BRITT *sits.*)

CHRIS: Thank you for the appointment. I'm happy to take this meeting.

BRITT: Tell me what you've brought.

CHRIS: My product will speak for itself.

BRITT: It speaks?

CHRIS: It can.

BRITT: The product talks?

CHRIS: Yes, but, my point is—

BRITT: There's a speaker, a microphone?

CHRIS: There's no speaker or a microphone. Please. Let me explain. The technical elements of the product—

BRITT: The "technical elements"?

CHRIS: Of the product. Yes.

(A pause)

BRITT: I don't meet with people often.

CHRIS: I'd heard, yes, and as I stated, thank you for the appointment.

BRITT: You heard I don't meet with people. You heard that from Francis.

CHRIS: Yes. I did.

BRITT: Francis sicced you on me.

CHRIS: "Sicced"?

BRITT: Francis *turned* you onto me. Francis put your shimmy into my court. *(Beat)* What did Francis say I could do for you?

CHRIS: Only that you could chat with me. That I could present you with my product. That we could discuss my product and its stunning implications and possibilities.

BRITT: "My experienced opinion." I bet Francis used those words, "Go and get Britt's experienced opinion."

CHRIS: Yes, Francis did use those words.

BRITT: "The person fit for the job." I bet Francis said that, too. About me. That I was "fit for the job." *(Beat)* Francis says a lot of shit. I mean, I've never met Francis in person, alive and in the flesh, but pardon my cursing, but holy hell, Francis does say a lot of shit.

Francis. That shit-talker. That ragaroll. *(Beat)* How do you know Francis?

CHRIS: Francis and I are neighbors. That's how we met. I've only spoken to Francis a few times, and only across the hedge outside my house. I've also never met Francis face to face. But Francis seems friendly. Cheerful.

BRITT: And why didn't Francis—

CHRIS: Francis told me this sort of thing was more your sort of thing. Even though I'd not even described what it was beyond my product being "magnificent." Francis thought, under the circumstances, with what's happening outside your gate—

BRITT: The circumstances are what they are.

CHRIS: Francis thought something "magnificent" might be just what you need.

BRITT: I see.

CHRIS: So Francis thought coming to you would be best.

BRITT: And Francis hasn't evaluated your product?

CHRIS: Francis hasn't.

BRITT: And Francis hasn't seen it?

CHRIS: Francis has not.

BRITT: And yet Francis pushed you this-a way.

CHRIS: I wasn't pushed.

BRITT: Suggested? Coerced? Aligned? How would you describe how Francis has placed the two of us together?

(A beat)

CHRIS: If we're going to play games—

BRITT: Games?

CHRIS: If I'm here on a lark—

BRITT: Pardon?

CHRIS: If this is a back-and-forth—

BRITT: Is that what you think this is? A back-and-forth?

CHRIS: Because my product—

BRITT: Is "stunning". "Magnificent." *"Like nothing I've seen before."*

CHRIS: Yes, in fact. It's like nothing you've ever seen.

(A pause. BRITT *looks out the window.)*

BRITT: What is your opinion? What is your opinion on what's happening outside our gates? *(Gestures out the window)* Look now at the rising smoke. What do you think of that? The rise of the smoke?

CHRIS: A shame.

BRITT: A shame?

CHRIS: That it is the way it is.

BRITT: Those tight-shirts outside the fences, screaming from the embankments, yelling from our lawns. I wonder what is in their brains? It makes me shiver. Thinking about it. All of it has made me very nerved-up, these tight shirts, their screaming, their accusations. I'm not bothered more than the low amount. I'm not bothered but my sleep has paid the price. I sleep like this *(Eyes open wide, head twisted sideways)* most nights. Nothing doing, I can't catch a break. I've insomnia from the slight irritation of it all.

CHRIS: I also had insomnia, years ago. But I've mastered it. I count backwards from ten.

(BRITT *stares at* CHRIS. *A pause)*

BRITT: Where did you grow up?

CHRIS: Where? Near here.

BRITT: Is there something in your upbringing?

CHRIS: In my upbringing?

BRITT: Something in your upbringing that turned you toward the profession of inventor?

CHRIS: I prefer the term "creator".

(A beat)

BRITT: Okay. Creator.

CHRIS: Certainly there is something in my upbringing that encouraged it. More to the point, there was something in my individual point of view; my personal perception. That is most likely what brought me toward the profession of "creator".

BRITT: And what was that personal perception that brought you thus, do you imagine?

CHRIS: I suppose it was how I perceived the sky, the earth, the wind, the grass. How some persons speak, how some do not. The look on a person's face. The curve of a hairline. The footstep of a person in a hallway.

BRITT: Quite poetic, your perception.

CHRIS: No, my descriptors are poetic. My perception is grounded in science. Those things I described and other things up to this, all of those things I've just said, en total, I've poured wholly into my product. A product I believe will revolutionize every aspect of our every being.

(CHRIS, standing, puts a gentle hand upon the box. BRITT smiles. BRITT's telephone rings. BRITT gestures to CHRIS to pause a moment, then BRITT quickly picks up the phone.)

BRITT: *(To phone)* Sam, yes... Monkeys. Cushions? From the... Back—red? Blue? Green? Out of green? Jesus, then, what, blue? Blue. Blue. Tell 'em. Tell 'em. *(Pause)* Blue. *(Long pause)* Sam. No. Okay. My—my, yeah, my,

yeah, you're number one. Sam. Number one. *(Goodbye)*
Shhpay-ta, peeeng-pong-tcho-thai. *(Later, ping-pong.*
Hangs up the phone) What color do you prefer for
random sequencers?

CHRIS: Do you mean dice?

BRITT: *Random sequencers.* Sam, on the phone, Sam was
asking about *random sequencers.* Generally speaking,
what color do you prefer?

(A beat)

CHRIS: I prefer plain white random sequencers.

BRITT: You know random sequencers were originally
made of teeth in ancient times. Teeth. Human teeth. If
random sequencers hadn't been made from teeth, then
the color could have been anything, anything at all.

(A beat)

CHRIS: I would very much like to begin my product
presentation.

BRITT: Before you do, let me tell you a little about
myself. It feels the scales are a bit imbalanced, me
having just heard so much about you and now you
knowing so little about me. So sit. Please sit.

(A pause. CHRIS sits.)

BRITT: A long time ago when I was young I had an
idea and the idea was this: I love to be… Since I was
young…I was surrounded by…

(A pause)

CHRIS: You've fulfilled your destiny.

BRITT: I did what?

CHRIS: You've fulfilled your life-long destiny,
continuing your family line, working here, developing
products, opening a horizon of wonder to humanity.

BRITT: Please don't interrupt me.

CHRIS: I'm sorry, but I've not got all day.

BRITT: No?

CHRIS: No. I don't.

(A pause)

BRITT: I don't like your condensensioned tone.

CHRIS: "Condensension?"

BRITT: Condenseeding ways of condifying. Perhaps Francis jumped the gun regarding our mutual introduction.

CHRIS: Perhaps Francis did jump the gun.

BRITT: So you're saying Francis jumped a gun?

CHRIS: I'm saying what?

BRITT: *That Francis has a gun?*

CHRIS: No, what?

(BRITT *stands.*)

BRITT: *(Pointed)* You're telling me *Francis has a gun*?

(BRITT *picks up the phone and pushes a button.* BRITT *turns away from* CHRIS.)

CHRIS: Wait, wait a minute—

BRITT: *(To phone)* Sam?—Francis? With Francis… Did you know anything about…a gun?? *(Pause)* No. This— *(Pause)* But was it meant as—? Is Francis…? No. No. Be alert. *(Pause)* I'm tired of—! *(Pause)* No. Sam. You're a—. Let me… *(Turns back toward* CHRIS*)* Okay. Sam. Yes. Thanks. *(Goodbye)* how-zie-jin, schlam-puh *(Okay. Bye, slut. Hangs up.)*

CHRIS: I'm sorry, I think we are through.

BRITT: We're through?

CHRIS: I think this meeting might have been a waste of my time.

BRITT: I'm sorry if you are offended.

CHRIS: If you only knew what I was about to present to you—

BRITT: Please, Chris—

CHRIS: If you would only listen, but you won't, to your detriment.

BRITT: You're right. I apologize. Please sit.

CHRIS: *NO!*

BRITT: How long have you known Francis?

CHRIS: Not long, but I have known Francis longer than I've known you. Understand? So with that, I'll be going.

(A beat. CHRIS *crosses toward the door.)*

BRITT: It's wild out there. In the world. In this climate. Walking out that door, you should realize your position.

CHRIS: I do realize my position. It is *you* who—

BRITT: Corporate product purchase and development is a super-fuck-cluster. The money and the time makes for big decision-making, so to just sign you on willy-nilly makes no sense. We must sit. We must chat. We must *learn* from each other and *that*, you must understand, is how deals are made. So I ask. Sit down please.

CHRIS: No. I'm upset and angry.

BRITT: Sit down.

CHRIS: I won't sit down. You are not in control of me.

BRITT: Please sit down.

CHRIS: I'm no longer comfortable with this product demonstration meeting! I am going to leave so thank you!

BRITT: You're no longer comfortable? When were
you at all *ever* comfortable? When is any person fully
comfortable? While asleep? Are you sleeping, Chris?
Am I? Are we sleeping? No. We're up. We're out
of bed. We're as awake as chickens. We're moving
and alive, bock bock bock. Our eyes are lit with the
glimmer of a thousand and twenty suns. So please
sit down. Let me try and ease your whatever it is. Let
me try and settle your whatever you got, whatever's
making you peevish, whatever's making you
wary, whatever's making your eyes do that thing.
Honestly—I am excited about this. I am excited to
talk to you. I am excited about your product. Your
"take charge" persona makes me believe you perhaps
have a possible wonder of a whatever. You've got my
imagination fired, can't you tell, I think. You've got my
interest peaked, can't you see, maybe. You've got me
salivating, pardon my drool, right, it could be true?

(A pause)

CHRIS: I apologize for my anger just before. My temper.
It was uncalled for. To yell at you as I did was not
right. I sincerely apologize. Please forgive me.

BRITT: No apology really necessary.

CHRIS: It is necessary. So I say. I'm sorry.

BRITT: No sorry really needed.

CHRIS: It is only that I believe my product is a life-
changer and this belief is heavily tied to my current
emotional state.

BRITT: I don't deny you believe what you've just now
said about your belief regarding how you feel about
your heavy ties to your emotional state.

CHRIS: Good.

BRITT: Know that I am on your side.

CHRIS: Thank you.

BRITT: As if we were fighters fighting fights together. Unified.

CHRIS: Okay.

BRITT: So. Here. Sit. Square one. We begin anew. I'm me. You're you. What else can we do?

(A pause. CHRIS *returns to the chair and sits.)*

BRITT: I want you to meet someone. *(Picks up phone) (To phone)* Sam? Come up here. *(Hangs up phone)* Sam will be coming up. I want the two of you to meet. *(To door)* Come in, Sam!

*(*SAM *enters.* SAM *wears a purple lab coat and wears a paper "clean room" hat.* SAM *swallows loudly and strangely while speaking.)*

SAM: Yes?

BRITT: Sam—

SAM: *(Steps forward)* Hello.

BRITT: *(To* CHRIS*)* Introduce yourself.

(A pause)

CHRIS: My name is Chris.

SAM: I...am...Sam.

CHRIS: Good to meet you, Sam.

SAM: *(To* BRITT*)* A...new...product?

BRITT: Yes.

SAM: Britt?

BRITT: *(To* SAM*)* Things are churning. Exciting, high times, fun fun fun.

SAM: *(Points at the box)* Is...that—

CHRIS: This?

SAM: What...is—?

CHRIS: It's my product.

SAM: Pro...duct.

BRITT: *(To* CHRIS*)* Let me introduce you—

CHRIS: But we've just met—

BRITT: No, I want to introduce you to *what it takes.* Sam? Remove your hat, turn around and show Chris what it takes.

(SAM *removes the hat and turns toward* CHRIS, *back facing* CHRIS. *The back of* SAM's *head is covered in twisting, puffy scar tissue that clumps as it runs down the back.* CHRIS, *startled, lets in a quick breath.)*

BRITT: Boy howdy. Am I wrong? And that's not insulting Sam. Sam knows it's a "boy howdy," and has said "boy howdy" more than a few times.

(SAM *puts on the cap and faces* CHRIS.)

BRITT: *(To* SAM*)* Thanks, Sam. *(Goodbye)* moo-kaab-zigh-tish-tennis-shhpay-ta-mit-pizza *(Meet me later by the ping-pong table with pizza).*

SAM: Verpiss...DICH, Pee-yen! *(Fuck you, asshole)*

BRITT: Yemik-mine-schvaz, chee chee. *(Eat cock, piece of trash).*

(SAM *exits.)*

CHRIS: What happened to that person?

BRITT: Sam did what it takes. Sam metaphorically and literally dove into the deep end of an empty swimming pool without a net. *(Pause)* Are you that kind of sort? Would you dive into the empty swimming pool without a net? Do you have "what it takes"?

CHRIS: I don't agree with how you quantify "what it takes".

BRITT: Then how would you quantify it?

CHRIS: Obviously not in the same way as you.

BRITT: How long have you developing your product?

CHRIS: Quite some time.

BRITT: Years?

CHRIS: Yes.

BRITT: The clock ticking, the months blurring past.

CHRIS: Yes.

BRITT: Your sacrifices: Time? Energy? Money? Love? Children? Relationships?

CHRIS: All those things. Yes.

BRITT: Would you agree that those things are abstractions?

CHRIS: Abstractions?

BRITT: What I'm asking is what have *you physically* sacrificed?

CHRIS: Physically?

BRITT: You can go on and on, endorse your product with high praise until you are a jumble but until I see the sacrifice, until it has physical manifestation—

CHRIS: Like that person?

BRITT: Sam.

CHRIS: So—

BRITT: Look at my hand. *(Raises hand, spreading fingers)* These three fingers, destroyed. Cut to the nub, burned to the core. These are new fingers, Chris. Brand new. They seem regular, but they're not. They're a different person's. A mystery whose they are. I had them attached. But the originals are gone. Because of my sacrifice. These are new fingers.

CHRIS: So you request bodily damage on my part.

BRITT: Everyone says people in my line of work are devils. They say it's hypocritical for us not to know who we must be. But my life is a series of flummoxes. Things are always herky-jerky here. I'm nerved-up as I'd told you when you first arrived. Wouldn't you be, in my shoes? I've got to be. It could mean my life. My throat could be cut. Not by you. But by those outside. Did you read any of the signs those tight-shirts are holding out there? Most of what those signs say aren't wrong. An exaggeration, but not wrong entirely. "A thousand deaths equals a million dollars." That one is there. That one is true. But that, in itself, is not entirely accurate. True but not accurate. Then there is, "The World has become humankind's rancid dung hill!" And then, "Chemicals create Devolution. STOP THE MURDER!" And "Earth weeps for the Slaughtered!" You understand?

CHRIS: My product, my product will affect *everyone* no matter who is inside *or* outside whatever "gate." Whatever "murder." Whatever "slaughter," whatever "chemicals," whatever "rancid dung hill." It will affect everyone, no matter background or means and the affect will be full, total and complete. And *no one,* no part of *anyone shall be sacrificed.*

(BRITT *stares at* CHRIS. *A pause. A loud explosion sounds outside. The lights flicker.* CHRIS *flinches, hard.* BRITT *stands as a statue.*)

BRITT: I need to make a quick call. (*Picks up the telephone. To phone*) Sam? Please come in here for a moment.

(SAM *enters.*)

SAM: Britt.

BRITT: I'm going to quickly get some air.

CHRIS: But—

BRITT: *I need some goddamn air!*

SAM: Certain…ly.

BRITT: Cam you stay here for a moment with Chris?

CHRIS: Britt—

SAM: Certain…ly I can…stay.

BRITT: *(To* CHRIS*)* I'm wrapped tight like a bundle. A bundle with tape wrapped tightly around and around and around. I need to get some air. I need to *fucking breathe.* So. I say: Stay put. Don't move. I smile.

*(*BRITT *smiles. A beat.* BRITT *exits. A pause.* SAM *shuts the door and locks it with a key.* SAM *stares at* CHRIS*. A pause)*

SAM: What's the product?

CHRIS: What?

SAM: I asked you about the product.

CHRIS: You're talking—

SAM: Normal. Yes.

CHRIS: But you're—

SAM: The breathing, it's just for Britt, for Britt's benefit. The breathing enhances certain aspects, adds to my "allure" as an employee. This mess *(Points at head)*, is as real as death itself. But the other stuff, the breathing, the stiff-leg walk, the spaz-talk, the crazy-eye—it's all just for show, so as to be looked upon as a high-end stooge, to be considered a member of the gold-standard within our shambling workforce.

CHRIS: Why did you lock the door?

SAM: Company policy. Company secrets being leaked and all of that. We have to lock doors. It's about responsibility. You understand. *(Pause)* While we wait, would you like to know the story of how I ended up this way?

CHRIS: That's not necessary.

SAM: *(Angered)* It's not?

CHRIS: It's not my business to know how you ended up this way.

SAM: I'm sure Britt mentioned a few details.

CHRIS: Britt mentioned enough.

SAM: I was concaved.

CHRIS: You were concaved. I see.

SAM: Yes. It was a ball. Not like "it was a ball" like it was "a glorious fun time" but it was a *ball* as in it was a ball like a bouncy ball like a ball you would throw, bounce, toss or catch. It was a toy. A rare toy. An item hidden away on the "lost continent". You're familiar with the "lost continent"?

CHRIS: Yes.

SAM: I was cutting through the landscape, amid the overturned busses along the border, the wild outgrowths of thorny maple and deadly spruce, along the sheer clifffalls of oily black obsidian and there I found, surrounded by a circular river of fire, the rare toy, the rare *ball* perched on a precipice. Brightly airbrushed pink and covered with white stars, it was perfect—just as the legends fortold. Many had tried to remove the ball but I was determined. In fact, it was more than just determined—it was my corporate obligation. So I grabbed a random and long length of fiberglass pipe and pole-vaulted across the river of fire and grasped the edge of the precipice. Turning myself, I grabbed my prize and as I did, the ground gave way and I spun into the circular river of fire. Luckily the river was very narrow at the spot where I had spun and only seventy percent of my body was horribly burned. But I did retrieve the ball. And now it dwells here, tucked away within the company's guarded vaults, safe for future generations. So I am a hero. And I'll remain a hero long as I keep up the act. You won't out me, will you? You won't spill that I'm not as tremendously damaged as Britt would like to think?

CHRIS: I won't out you. No.

SAM: Good. Thanks. *(Pause)* Let me ask, if you don't mind—what's your opinion? Of what is going out outside, the tight-shirts at the gate? What do you think of them screaming about the torture of our current on-staff malformed creatures?

CHRIS: So are you saying it's true?

SAM: Is it true there are malformed creatures here? Yes. It's true. They are the "children".

CHRIS: Children? The children are malformed?

SAM: Wait.

CHRIS: What?

SAM: I've said too much.

CHRIS: The tight-shirts are right about the "chemicals"?

SAM: So you side with the tight-shirts?

(A beat)

CHRIS: I don't side with one faction or the other. I'm an independent.

(A pause)

SAM: That's smart. You're smart. I can tell you're smart. Smart people are sometimes useful. You're taking a great risk coming here, you know that, don't you. *(Pause)* You've been holed up?

CHRIS: I have been, yes.

SAM: Developing your product?

CHRIS: Yes. For years.

SAM: I was like you once. Before my sacrifice. I was once you. But no longer. Now there is upheaval. *(Pause)* May I trust you with another secret? Riots abound. Not only outside. But *inside*. Inside the company itself. And I'll leave it at that. You can gather the rest. You can put two and two together. "The truth shall set you free."

CHRIS: What do you mean by that?

SAM: "The truth…" *(Begins breathing strangely once more)* "…shall set…you free."

(BRITT enters.)

BRITT: Hello, Chris. I'm back. I'm better. I hope everything was all right with Sam. Thank you, Sam for waiting, thank you Sam. That will be all, Sam. Back down to the gates. That will be all.

SAM: Yes…Britt. As…you…wish.

BRITT: *(Goodbye)* Biz bald pen-day-ho *(Later, jackass)*.

(A beat. SAM exits.)

BRITT: Give me your product prototype presentation.

CHRIS: Right now?

BRITT: Yes.

CHRIS: All right.

BRITT: I'm feeling refreshed now. *(Beat)* Francis was the person who sent you here?

CHRIS: Francis was the person, yes.

BRITT: So let's hear what you've got.

CHRIS: Is everything okay—?

BRITT: Yes, so—

CHRIS: So I should—

BRITT: Do you need me to sit anyplace specific?

CHRIS: Oh, um—

BRITT: Where would you like me?

(A pause)

CHRIS: Sit. There.

(BRITT *moves slightly.)*

BRITT: Here?

CHRIS: That's fine, too, I suppose.

BRITT: Then here I sit. *(Sits)*

CHRIS: I'm happy to begin now.

BRITT: Then begin. *(Beat)* What did you and Sam talk about?

CHRIS: Sam?

BRITT: Yes.

CHRIS: Oh. Nothing. Much.

BRITT: Well. Fair enough.

CHRIS: Okay. First, do you mind if I—

BRITT: Say a few things? Please do.

(CHRIS *digs a piece of notebook paper from a pocket.* CHRIS *glances over the notes.)*

CHRIS: I appreciate you. Seeing me today. So I can present you with what I'm about to present...to...you. This amazing thing. A life-changer. As I've stated. Um. *(Pause)* I've suddenly lost my brain.

BRITT: Huzzah! Rally forth!

(A pause)

CHRIS: All right. Today...today we look upon our world as a place of vast difference, when in reality our "everyday" is more the same than divergent. If we were to place our "everyday" under a microscope, to put it on a slide and look at it, from close up and far away, we would see two separate existences. The existence that is far would be a blue and green blob. The existence that is close would be atoms stretching across atoms to form a toothbrush. Are you following?

BRITT: Certainly.

CHRIS: Great. Great. *Great*. So with the degrees in which perception is given, we as a world are shortsighted, missing the greater outlook on what is and what surrounds us. Take for example our outdoors. Or, along with that, generally speaking, "technology". Or procreation. Or farming and for that matter, eating and sustaining health so that life is good and life continues. *(Beat)* What degree of perception is there daily?

(A pause)

BRITT: Is that rhetorical?

CHRIS: No.

BRITT: So—

CHRIS: What degree of perception is there daily?

BRITT: Oh. Um. Little degree of perception?

CHRIS: Yes! Right! Little degree.

BRITT: There is little degree of perception daily.

CHRIS: Yes. Of the small things. What lies below. What lies beneath. What we encounter must be shown to us, we must be able to relate on a one-to-one level with our own daily existence.

BRITT: So your prototype—

CHRIS: Right. My prototype—

BRITT: Is it—?

CHRIS: Please reserve further questions until the presentation is complete.

BRITT: Sorry.

CHRIS: Sorry. It will all be clear soon. This build-up is necessary for what I am about to present. You'll understand when you see. And when you see…you'll understand. *(Pause)* Inside this box, inside this box is something that will not only change your perception of daily life—

BRITT: But—

CHRIS: Please reserve—

BRITT: This is—

CHRIS: Please reserve—

BRITT: This is a question for clarification—

CHRIS: Oh. Then. Please. Continue.

BRITT: You just said that what you have will change my perception of daily life and then before that you said we had no *perception* of daily life.

CHRIS: No, I asked what degree of perception of daily life there is.

BRITT: And I said…?

CHRIS: Little perception.

BRITT: Oh. Right.

CHRIS: So—

BRITT: Sorry. Continue.

CHRIS: You will have felt foolish in a moment for that question. Not that you're a fool. Only. Just… *(Beat)* What I have in this box will change your perception. And by that, I mean fully. Fully change. Everything. All of it. From hand to foot, from sea to cosmos, from sand to paper.

BRITT: And it will uniquely change my daily perception?

CHRIS: It will blow your top. Tops will blow.

BRITT: Go on.

CHRIS: Within this box is all that ever shall be. Within this box is what the Hindi once called "Zindagi".

BRITT: "Zindagi"?

CHRIS: I must ask you to not make sudden movements. I must ask you not to flail around as you are astounded by what is contained here. I must ask you to not disbelieve, counter-repremand or poo-poo outright.

BRITT: How can I agree to—

CHRIS: *Agree to my terms or I walk out the door.*

BRITT: I agree to your terms.

CHRIS: Behold. I will open the box and remove the product. Behold what astonishment I bring. *(Beat)* I'll need an input. Do you have an input?

BRITT: An optical input?

CHRIS: Yes.

BRITT: On the table.

(CHRIS *hooks a wire from the table and hooks it up to a small digital camera.*)

CHRIS: Where does—

(BRITT *pushes a button on a wall, revealing a closed-circuit television behind a hidden wall panel.*)

CHRIS: Thank you.

(CHRIS *removes five small people-shaped "dolls" from the box.* CHRIS *sets them on their "feet" and aims the small camera at them as the television flickers, showing the dolls close-up. The dolls appear quite human.*)

(A pause)

CHRIS: One moment. It takes a bit, one moment. Wait and watch. Shh. Watch and see.

(A long pause. The small "dolls" begin to move in a very "alive" way.)

BRITT: Shit my pants. Shit my pants shit my pants—

CHRIS: "Zindagi."

BRITT: Shit my pants.

CHRIS: "Zindagi." It means—

BRITT: "Life." "Zindagi" means "life".

CHRIS: Yes.

BRITT: They're alive.

CHRIS: Of course.

BRITT: So small.

CHRIS: Yes.

BRITT: Look at them.

CHRIS: Did I exaggerate?

BRITT: My god. *(Reaching for one of the "dolls")* Let me hold one—

CHRIS: Whoa, whoa whoa—you'll hurt them if you grab at them. Their bodies are made from melded tissue, grafted bone, hydroxoplasma—

BRITT: Tissue, bone and hydroxoplasma?

CHRIS: And a hundred other ingredients that only I know how to combine.

BRITT: So they're fragile?

CHRIS: As fragile as you or I.

BRITT: How old are they?

CHRIS: They begin at thirty years old or forty years old or so.

BRITT: What do they eat?

CHRIS: Chicken. Soup. Corn. Pizza. Ice Cream. Tofu.

BRITT: And their clothes?

CHRIS: Sweaters and pants and shoes and socks and underpants.

BRITT: Reproduction?

CHRIS: Yes.

BRITT: Language?

CHRIS: Yes.

BRITT: Are they aware we stand above them?

CHRIS: Yes. Very much.

(CHRIS *waves at the "dolls." The "dolls" wave back.)*

BRITT: Shit my pants. *(Pause)* Life.

CHRIS: "Zindagi."

BRITT: Astounding.

CHRIS: Yes.

BRITT: And you say they speak?

(BRITT *leans an ear toward the "dolls".)*

CHRIS: Yes.

BRITT: I can't understand—

CHRIS: Listen carefully—

(BRITT *listens.)*

BRITT: Did I hear one just ask for "a snack"?

CHRIS: They do like their snacks.

(BRITT *stands straight and stares at* CHRIS.)

BRITT: What are you calling them?

CHRIS: The whole thing?

BRITT: Yes.

CHRIS: Including a future realized play-set and "take care tools," and a separate "cleaning station." The product's name is "*Microcosm*".

(A pause)

BRITT: Would an endless flow of money be enough for you?

CHRIS: An endless—

BRITT: As if money were no longer money, that everything you ever desired were free because cost would not matter because cost would not exist.

CHRIS: That's a lot of money.

BRITT: It's not really money, at that point, is it? Clarifying. Money would not be money.

CHRIS: Money is good, but I'm unsure, I'm unsure if you understand what I'm bringing to you.

BRITT: I understand what you bring to me. Fully. I see what this is. So you tell me what you want.

CHRIS: I'm not abandoning the money, mind you. It's just. What I've brought changes the direction of human existence. Therefore, I would like to be included in the marketing and development process. And I would need final say.

BRITT: On?

CHRIS: Everything. My word would be the last word. Period.

BRITT: This is my company, Chris. I have final say. I've always had final say. That's the way this company has endured, with my final say. Even with a product such as yours. I must have final say. It's the only way I do business.

CHRIS: Unacceptable.

BRITT: Understand my position. You would have extreme input. But not final say.

CHRIS: I'd be giving up too much.

BRITT: Hardly.

CHRIS: Far too much. You must understand.

BRITT: Tell me your favorite.

CHRIS: Favorite?

BRITT: Of our line. Tell me your favorite. It can be from anytime. From long ago. From today. I just want to prove to you there's a method to my madness. And I think you'll be impressed. And to impress a creator... That's just sound business. *(Beat)* All right. I've something I'd like to show you. Please put your product aside for a moment.

(A beat)

CHRIS: All right.

(CHRIS scoops up the "dolls" and returns them to the box. He turns off the camera.)

BRITT: Good. Now. Tell me your favorite.

CHRIS: I'm still confused.

BRITT: Of our line. Your favorite. Your favorite from when you were a child.

CHRIS: Oh. I see. My favorite. *(Pause)* "The Seascaper."

BRITT: "The Seascaper." That's stretching back quite a bit.

CHRIS: It was an innovative winner and imminently playable.

BRITT: It was.

CHRIS: The schemes were far ahead of their time.

BRITT: Very true. No doubt, Chris. You *know your stuff.* *(A beat. BRITT crosses to the front door and touches it.)* Heat-sensored lock. Very secure. Door made from corrugated Venilium. Very secure. A secure room. You'll soon see why. (BRIOTT *crosses to one of the cabinets. Removing some keys from a pocket,* BRITT *unlocks the cabinet. From within,* BRITT *removes a dusty plastic bag.)* 14-J. (BRITT *places the plastic bag on the table and closes the cabinet and locks it once more.* BRITT *crosses to the table and opens the bag.* BRITT *pulls a waxy model car from within.)*

CHRIS: Oh my god.

BRITT: 14-J. "The Seascaper."

CHRIS: Oh my god.

BRITT: Created by Jean Yiddles.

CHRIS: Almost sixty years ago.

BRITT: With diodes that read pulse-rate, thus mimicking the player's own body linguistics.

CHRIS: Yes.

BRITT: This is the prototype—

CHRIS: The original prototype?

BRITT: *The original prototype.*

CHRIS: Never in my life.

BRITT: I know, I know.

CHRIS: Never in my life would I have thought I would see this.

BRITT: It's nothing compared to your creation, I understand, but with this, our legacy is proven, the lineage of this company and my own beliefs can not be questioned. I do what's right. I protect the history and future of this company. I would unto my dying breath. And this model, this model of "The Seascaper" proves it. *(Pause)* Would you like to look at it on the table?

CHRIS: Yes. Very much. Thank you.

(BRITT *places the waxy car on the table. A pause*)

CHRIS: Is this the final rendition ?

BRITT: This is the original prototype. That's how perfect the original was. There was never a single modification after the original prototype. The original prototype and the final rendition *are the same thing*. That's how we do things here. *(Beat)* Would you like to hold it in your hands? I would allow it. Because I trust you. I believe in you. You are soon to be a team member, I hope. So do what you will. *(Beat)* I knew Jean Yiddles, you know. I was a child. Jean Yiddles. The creator of the "Seascopper". My parents would have Gene over for snacks. Gene's favorite snacks. Crackers and sausage. I ate sausage and crackers with Gene Yiddles. Yes. It's true. That was me. *(Pause)* Would you like to hold it?

CHRIS: Yes.

BRITT: Then do so.

(CHRIS *delicately picks up the waxy car.*)

BRITT: Very light but also heavy. Strong and flimsy. The first of our products mass produced on a scale of one billion. Over one billion. All from that. All from that original prototype slash final rendition. So you see? So you see why I must have final say? Why things go according to how they've always gone accordingly? *(Pause)* You feel Gene Yaddle's hand on the work? Gene's inspiration pulsing from the materials? It's a totem. What you hold is a totem. A totem deserving worship, needing sacrifices, the thing we pray to, the thing we stroke when times are difficult. You feel the solid power within it. And that can be your product, too. Times one-hundred-thousand. Your product will put Joan Yaddles to shame. Your product will be the shadow that overtakes. Your product will be the lasting cornerstone of a new world. Your product will be what all beings think of when they think, "miraculous." The old way is over.

(BRITT *takes the waxy car from* CHRIS.)

BRITT: A new day has dawned. (BRITT *smashes the waxy car with a fist. The car explodes into small, waxy shards.*) That is how much I believe.

CHRIS: You smashed it.

BRITT: Yes. I smashed it to bits.

CHRIS: Why did you do that?

BRITT: I feel I underestimagted you.

CHRIS: You—?

BRITT: I underestimaged everything about this meeting. We're very much the same, aren't we? As I said before? We're cut from similar cloth. You're a "young me." But I don't necessarily mean linear age. I mean currently you are a speck while I am a universe. You are a molecule while I am a mighty oak. You are a maggot while I am a titan. But you could be a titan yet. Or an oak. Or the universe. I can give you that. If you allow our partnership to take seed and grow. But if we are to join together in this endeavor, you must know my secrets. Those tight shirts at the gate. You want to know why they scream? Why they call for my head? This you'd like to know. This you will *need* to know. (BRITT *crosses to another cabinet.* BRITT *unlocks it and removes two pairs of plastic goggles, two pairs of bright rubber gloves and two "electro gas masks".*) You must do as I say. Put these on. Put on these goggles.

(*A pause.* CHRIS *puts on the goggles.*)

BRITT: Put on this electro gas mask.

(CHRIS *puts on the electro gas mask.*)

BRITT: Put on these rubber gloves.

(CHRIS *puts on the rubber gloves.*)

BRITT: Now flip the switch on the side of the electro gas mask.

(CHRIS *flips a small switch on the side of the mask.*)

BRITT: Say your name.

CHRIS: *(Strangely electro-like)* Chris. Chris Yaelenclaven. Chris.

BRITT: Working perfectly. (BRITT *puts on the goggles, gloves and electro gas mask. He flips a switch. Strangely electro-like*) Growth.

CHRIS: *(Still electro-like)* Rowth?

BRITT: Growth.

CHRIS: Growth.

BRITT: Yes.

CHRIS: Growth.

BRITT: Listen.

CHRIS: I am listening.

BRITT: We are about *growth*. (BRITT *crosses to another cabinet. Unlocking the cabinet, BRITT pulls out a metal box with a dangerous looking symbol painted on it. BRITT places the box on the table.*) An example: (BRITT *opens the box and dumps the contents on the table, a small pile of odd plastic toys.*) Look closely.

(CHRIS *stares closely at the small pile of toys.*)

CHRIS: My god.

BRITT: Yes.

CHRIS: What is the level of—

BRITT: High—

CHRIS: But—

BRITT: The level of adulteration—

CHRIS: How did this—

BRITT: The level of adulteration is very, very high.

(A pause)

CHRIS: Have you tongs?

(BRITT removes some tongs from a sock. BRITT hands CHRIS the tongs. CHRIS moves the tongs near the toys.)

BRITT: Gentle, gentle.

(CHRIS nods. CHRIS crosses to the small pile of toys and begins to moves the toys around.)

CHRIS: Incredible.

BRITT: The bluination is nearly invisible—

CHRIS: The bluinitve pattern—

BRITT: Noxious spectral shifting.

CHRIS: A bluinated spectral shift—

BRITT: Creating dimensional gasses—

CHRIS: This level of dimensional gasses would create—

BRITT: A heavy degree—

CHRIS: A massive dose would—

BRITT: Without the goggles, gloves and electro-gas mask, the result could be rectal implosion, lung needles, cranial spotting and heart shrinkage.

CHRIS: And on a larger scale—

BRITT: Far worse. The result is full body cellular dementia with an adolescent-form ending shift.

CHRIS: Malformation.

BRITT: Exactly. Malformation.

CHRIS: Crates and crates, together could create a situation—

BRITT: Twenty-four hour immediate malformity of the entire adult form and adult psyche into the pre-pubesent, adolescent form.

CHRIS: A regression from adult to child.

BRITT: Yes.

CHRIS: Cellular regression.

(A beat)

BRITT: Best I pack these up.

CHRIS: Oh yes. Of course.

(BRITT *packs the small toys back into the metal box and returns the box to the cabinet.)*

(CHRIS *begins to remove the electro gas mask.)*

BRITT: Stop! Wait!

(CHRIS *stops and waits.* BRITT *walks toward the window and opens it.)*

BRITT: Five... Four... Three... Two... One. Remove.

(BRITT *and* CHRIS *remove their goggles, gloves and electro gas masks.)*

(BRITT *holds out a trash can.)*

BRITT: Here.

(CHRIS *puts the goggles, gloves and electro gas mask in the trash can.* BRITT *does the same.)*

BRITT: The truth is the totality of the "crates and crates" of the subsequently contaminated and bluinatied product never left our overseas warehouse in the "lost continent" where the initial bluination took place.

CHRIS: The bluination was the cause of the malformations.

BRITT: Yes. So no federal emergency. The malformations, my company's factory workers employed as "mineral extractors" on the far-off "lost continent" —these exposed workers were quarantined and the subsequent bluinated product was never shipped to our customers. We were careful after what happened. The product remained in the warehouse. There was no exposure to the population at large. But we did recover, of course, this small batch of the bluinated product for testing purposes. So—what the tight-shirts are screaming about outside the gates? All partially true. But the larger perception? They truly fail to try and understand.

CHRIS: I see.

BRITT: So now you see the full order of business. Now you know the cost, the *sacrifice*. The infected crates— there was no way we could have known how severe those malformations would be. And legally we don't even call what happened to our workers on "the lost continent" an accident, but it was very "accidentish" to be sure. We've done what we can for those malformed people, every one of the malformed have been retained. They remain employed, right here in the building. The only rule we ask is that they stay on the floors below and keep themselves fit. Well. Fit enough. *(Pause)* So there you are. I've come clean. I would very much like to produce this product with you. I really would. I'm your number one fan. Believe it. And my proof will be in my putting.

(A long pause)

CHRIS: All right.

BRITT: All right?

CHRIS: Yes.

BRITT: We have a deal?

CHRIS: A deal. Yes. A deal.

(BRITT extends a hand. CHRIS shakes BRITT's hand.)

BRITT: You've made the right decision. I'll have legal draw up a contract. A formalized contract. But a handshake is as good as signed, am I right?

(BRITT *and* CHRIS *ultimately let go of each other's hands.*)

BRITT: A dream realized.

CHRIS: I'm a bit shaken up, pardon me. I feel the culmination of my life's work. I'm sorry. I've become emotional. This is a big deal for me. I'm sorry. I'm about to cry.

BRITT: You're showing your humanity. That's nothing to be ashamed of. I applaud you. (BRITT *applauds. A pause*) Chris.

CHRIS: Yes?

BRITT: Your product name. "Microcosm"?

CHRIS: Yes.

BRITT: To tell you frankly, I'm not happy with that name. Product names should not define the product within, but the feeling that the consumer gets when opening the product. The feeling that washed over me, and understand I've been in this business all my life, so what I'm saying is the name of this product should be something that the heart understands upon the brain receiving the impulse from the eyeballs. *(Pause)* You know how my parent came up with the name "Starscaper"?

CHRIS: I think you mean "Seascaper"?

BRITT: Do you know how my parent came up with that name? It's a toy car. With diodes that read pulse-rate, thus mimicking the player's own body linguistics. None of that says "Starscaper" to you, does it? But my parent, holding Jan's prototype—

CHRIS: *Jene's*—

BRITT: Jene Maddle's—

CHRIS: Jene *Yiddle's*—

BRITT: As my parent held the prototype in my parent's hand, my parent's mind remembered a time when my parent was riding the western sea on a large freighter, a five ton freighter filled to the brim with various mammal-fish and the ship was so over-laden with mammal-fish that one of the people on the ship, one of the mates, the mate said to my parent "This ship will scrape the bottom is it so over-laden with mammal-fish" And that stuck with my parent. So much so that when my parent held James Mandible's prototype of the "Shipscraper", my parent came up with that name. The "Shipscraper".

CHRIS: —"Seascaper."—

BRITT: And it's what my parent felt was right. And my parent was right. My parent's feelings led my parent there. And those same feelings tell me that your product, what it does to me is it places me above. Makes my perception into what your little creation's perception of what my perception might be. So if I were them, where I would live would not be a "microcosm." What we need to do is invert, establish, and confirm the true "necessity" of your product. How best it will be consumed by all of humanity. Because humanity will consume it. I make that a guarantee. So the new name. Let us define the product by ourselves, not by the product alone. So the name shall be "*Macrocosm*".

CHRIS: "Macrocosm."

BRITT: Yes.

CHRIS: Instead of—

BRITT: Your name. Because it's about us. Not them. It's not about those little things in the box. It's not about their lives. It's about *our* lives. *Us.* How they view us, not how we view them. We are the *"macrocosm"*, do you see? We're the sky. The clouds. The planets. The universe. The slash of lightning, the eye of judgement. We're their "macrocosm". You see?

CHRIS: Yes. I see.

BRITT: So. Now. First thing we should do is take your product to the lab and begin to break it down and rebuild it so as to jump-start manufacture, yes?

CHRIS: Break it down and rebuild it?

BRITT: I misspoke. On paper only. Not physically "break it down".

CHRIS: Oh. Good. All right.

BRITT: It's a new day for us here. Our blemishes will be erased. The screams outside our gates of "tyranny" and "death to corporate ragarolls" and "kill all who dwell within that holy hell of a corporation" will be replaced by voices of lovely gratitude. A new bright world where all is bright and new will begin, with you and me at the top of the heap. It is an honor to be on the ground floor of such an exciting new product. So. Again. *Thank you.* Or should I thank Francis? Francis. That bastard. I'll never thank Francis. Francis is scum. But stupid scum, ay? To let this one get away. It's a good joke fate has played. I laugh at Francis and fate has laughed, too, along with me laughing. The opportunity Francis has missed. The chance of a lifetime. A complete nondercudden. To choose to pass up such an opportunity. To unwittingly choose to pass up *life. (Pause)* May I see them one more time?

CHRIS: Once more?

BRITT: Once more before we take them to the lab. For prototype breakdown. Yes.

(A pause)

CHRIS: All right.

BRITT: Wonderful.

(CHRIS *opens the box and removes a few of the dolls. He aims the camera at the dolls. They again appear on the closed circuit television. The dolls interact.*)

CHRIS: They appear somewhat nervous.

BRITT: Is that right?

CHRIS: They have limited emotion drivers, but they do have a core of the typical reactionary singulators.

BRITT: They seem to be staring at us.

CHRIS: They do. Yes.

BRITT: Why are they doing that?

CHRIS: Maybe they're locked to the sounds of our voices. Or the sounds outside the gates are subjugating their water cores. I'll need to do some testing.

BRITT: Could they have heard what we've discussed?

CHRIS: Their capacity for processing language is quite limited.

BRITT: Can you make them dance?

CHRIS: Dance? (*Beat*) Of course.

(BRITT *pushes a small button on* BRITT's *watch. Tinny music plays. The creatures dance.*)

BRITT: Delightful! Better than I can do!

CHRIS: They're quick to learn.

BRITT: Catchy!

(BRITT *begins to dance.* CHRIS *begins to dance.* BRITT *turns up the volume on* BRITT's *watch. The creatures stop and begin to watch* BRITT *and* CHRIS.)

(Suddenly, a large vent cover blows away from one of the walls and crashes to the floor. BRITT and CHRIS freeze in their tracks. BRITT turns off BRITT's watch music.)

BRITT: Pick up the box and run.

CHRIS: What?

BRITT: PICK UP THE BOX AND RUN!

(From within the vent appears CAROL. CAROL is dressed in a dirty purple jumpsuit. CAROL brandishes a long homemade knife and rushes toward BRITT as CHRIS quickly stuffs the "dolls" back into the box. CAROL puts the knife to BRITT's throat.)

CAROL: FLOOR!

BRITT: Don't slit my throat!

CAROL: *(To CHRIS)* FLOOR!

BRITT: I'm not moving a muscle! Don't slit my throat!

CAROL: *(To BRITT)* FLOOR FLOOR FLOOR!

BRITT: What floor are we on? Is that what you're asking us?

CAROL: FLOOR!

BRITT: Floor fifteen.

(A beat)

CAROL: Fifteen?

BRITT: Yes. Fifteen.

(A pause)

CAROL: Britt Nasheffer.

BRITT: No, no, no. You're mistaken.

CAROL: Fifteen! BRITT NASHEFFER!

BRITT: That's not me. *(Pointing at CHRIS)* That person is Britt Nasheffer, not I.

CHRIS: What?

CAROL: Is not Britt Nasheffer. You Britt Nahseffer.

BRITT: Is so Britt Nasheffer.

CHRIS: I'm not Britt Nasheffer!

CAROL: *(To* CHRIS*) Is not Britt Nasheffer!*

CHRIS: What the holy hell is going on right now?!

(A pause. CAROL *shoves* BRITT *to the ground and points the blade at* BRITT.*)*

CAROL: Riot.

BRITT: Riot?

CHRIS: Riot?

CAROL: *Riot!*

BRITT: Who?

CAROL: Us!

CHRIS: Who?

BRITT: You?

CAROL: Yes!

CHRIS: Them?

BRITT: Where?

CAROL: Everywhere!

BRITT: Intending what?

CAROL: Extermination.

BRITT: Wait—

CAROL: Destruction. Ruination. Escape and retribution.

CHRIS: It's a child.

BRITT: This is not a child!

CHRIS: That is a child.

BRITT: No. It's one of them. It's a *malformation.*

CHRIS: A malformation? It can't be. It's too perfectly a child.

BRITT: That's not a child! That's a grown person! A cellularly degenerated grown person! A grown-up, malformed person! Believe your eyes if you like, but that's not a child!

CHRIS: *(To* CAROL*)* You're truly a malformed grown person?

CAROL: Who.

CHRIS: Who?

CAROL: *Who! You!*

CHRIS: Me. I'm Chris Yaelenclaven.

CAROL: Why here?

CHRIS: A meeting. I'm a product developer. It went well. A fabulous invention. But nothing's been signed. But we did shake hands and I'd like to believe we're about to change the world for the better.

(An explosion shakes the building. CAROL *falls, the stands and points the blade once more.* CHRIS *kneels next to* BRITT.*)*

BRITT: I'd like to interject—

CAROL: What?

BRITT: None of this is directly my fault.

CAROL: *What?*

BRITT: If I'm to be killed—

CAROL: Where—

BRITT: What we've done to the likes of you—

CAROL: What?

BRITT: To your minds, your bodies—

CAROL: Our—?

BRITT: You believe we've done it out of spite but accidents—

CAROL: Stand.

BRITT: Accidents happen in the workplace, no matter if it is in a corporate board room or a lost prehistoric jungle region on a lost continent. Accidents happen. The blame is not ours squarely. You must understand that we must break a few eggs, yes? For the good of humanity?

CAROL: *Stand!*

BRITT: Chris, too?

CAROL: *Stand!*

BRITT: *(To* CHRIS*)* We both should stand.

*(*BRITT *and* CHRIS *stand.)*

CAROL: Stuck.

BRITT: Stuck?

CAROL: You don't…want stuck.

BRITT: No.

CAROL: Hand.

BRITT: Hand?

CAROL: HAND! *(Swings the knife around)*

BRITT: *(To* CAROL*)* You don't need to swing that knife at us.

CAROL: Keys. In hand.

BRITT: What?

CAROL: *Keys! In hand!*

BRITT: Oh no. You're not getting my keys.

CAROL: Keys in hand or stuck in face!

BRITT: Try and stick me in the face or anywhere else and try and stick that person, too, and you just see what happens.

CHRIS: Wait—

BRITT: Stick both of us in the guts, pull out our intestines, draw them on the floor, take your revenge on us for only doing our duty, only trying to change life as anyone would know it! Blame us for being idealists, for trying to make the entirety of humanity sustainable and happy! Stick us and get what you think you deserve!

CAROL: Keys keys keys keys!

BRITT: *(To* CHRIS*)* Part of the affect of the chemical malformation. This pouting. This aggrandizing. A bitter hatred of progress of any kind. An animosity that leaves only a frightened, shouting malformed person-child without hope for the future. But I've been schooled. Watch this now. *(Using a "kid voice", to* CAROL*)* Give me the blade.

CAROL: No. Keys.

BRITT: Give me the blade.

CAROL: No! Keys!

BRITT: Tradesies?

(A pause)

CAROL: Tradesies?

BRITT: Knuckle-down tradesies.

CAROL: Even-stevens?

BRITT: Yes.

CAROL: Even tradesies?

BRITT: Yes. I said. Yes.

CAROL: Swear?

BRITT: Triple swear.

CAROL: Pinky deal.

BRITT: Pinky deal.

(BRITT and CAROL pinky swear.)

CAROL: On three.

BRITT: On three.

CAROL: No give backs?

(A pause. BRITT drops the "kid voice".)

BRITT: No give backs.

CAROL: Honest to die?

BRITT: Honest to die.

(BRITT and CAROL share a quick, elaborate handshake to seal the deal.)

BRITT: On my count. *(Removes a ring of keys from jacket.)*

CAROL: Go.

BRITT: Three…two…one…

(BRITT holds out keys and CAROL holds out the knife. Both trade items quickly. A pause)

BRITT: *(To CHRIS)* Mistakes abound.

(CAROL moves toward the vent. BRITT rushes to block CAROL's path, holding the knife before CAROL.)

BRITT: *(To CAROL)* Mistakes mistakes. A bad trade, my good person. I'm so sorry, but a very bad trade.

(CAROL throws the keys into the open vent. A pause)

BRITT: Well shitty shit shit. You just did a terrible thing. Those keys were more valuable than you'd probably ever realize. Or maybe you do realize. Either way, you'll learn your lesson—

CHRIS: Britt—

BRITT: We need those keys.

CHRIS: What for?

BRITT: To get into rooms! This is a corporation, for god's sake!

CHRIS: If you'd stop to consider—

BRITT: Consider—?

CHRIS: A rational response—

BRITT: Chris! Do you want your product on shelves in the next four to six months or not?! Do you not want to begin development and product design? Do you not want "Megacosm"—

CHRIS: "Megacosm?"

BRITT: —in the hands of every human on the earth—

CHRIS: —but I thought—

BRITT: —as soon as possible so that others—

CHRIS: —you said it now called "*Macro*cosm"—

BRITT: —may enjoy "*Megacosm*" as I have, with a smile on my face and a jump in my heart? Do you want "Megacosm" to be the item that finally brings our lowly planet together as one? Do you want "Megacosm" to be the one thing the entire population can look upon and know they now need no Gods because they are now gods themselves will then become more giving, loving and beneficent?

CHRIS: Yes. Of course I want that. That's why I came here today.

BRITT: Then allow me to get to the business of murdering this ungrateful malformed child -person factory slave so that wonder and hope will spill anew on this planet's next horizon.

CHRIS: I think that maybe, perhaps there could be another alternative you could take than homicide.

BRITT: And that, dear Chris, is why you'd never make good upper management material.

(BRITT *approaches* CAROL.)

(*A missile flies through the open window and spirals through the room, imbedding itself into a wall.*)

(CAROL *pulls a chair down to the floor and ducks behind it.*)

(*A pause*)

CHRIS: That's…wow…look…it's…

BRITT: A missile.

CHRIS: A missile.

BRITT: Shh shh—

CHRIS: A missile a missile, somebody shot a missile at us! It's going to explode!

BRITT: I would have thought it would have exploded by now.

CHRIS: It's a missile!

BRITT: And not the best one I've seen, not the best by far.

CHRIS: What should we do?

BRITT: Do?

CHRIS: I'm unsure how to proceed. I've never had a missile shot at me before.

BRITT: Get used to it.

CHRIS: Get used to it?

BRITT: It happens to me daily. And since you're part of the team now, it would be good for you to get used missiles being shot at you.

CHRIS: Oh god.

(BRITT *removes* BRITT's *phone from a pocket.*)

CHRIS Wait! You're going to make the missile explode!

BRITT: The odds are miniscule my phone's cellular static will make this missile explode. Missiles are like snowflakes. Each one different with its own unique personality. So its best to act normally and if the odd explosion should happen, you go with the flow.

CHRIS: That's your advice?

BRITT: We have a procedure in place in case of missile.

CHRIS: What procedure?

BRITT: I call Sam.

CHRIS: But—

BRITT: What happens if the missile explodes before I call Sam? Then we all die together. Including Megacosm. All three of us will be joined together in ash, bone and blood.

CHRIS: I need to protect Megacosm.

BRITT: All right. *(Picks up the box)*

CHRIS: WHAT ARE YOU DOING!? DON'T SHAKE THE MEGACOSM! ARE YOU A CRAZY PERSON?

(CHRIS *takes the box from* BRITT.)

BRITT: I'm not crazy. I'm sane. So do not worry. We're safe as houses.

(BRITT *gently places the box on the table.)*

BRITT: Nothing will happen to Megacosm. I promise. I give you my word

(SAM *enters.* SAM *looks like* SAM's *been through a firefight.* SAM *carries a missile launcher.)*

BRITT: Sam.

SAM: I figured you all would be blown up by now.

CHRIS: Wait, is that a missile launcher? Are you the person who shot a missile at us?

SAM: Yes.

BRITT: This is surprising.

(CAROL *stands.*)

SAM: The malformation is not supposed to have come yet.

BRITT: It crawled up through the duct work.

SAM: *(To* CAROL*)* You were supposed to wait until the missile had exploded! You've done everything out of order.

CHRIS: *(To* SAM*)* Why did you shoot a missile at us!

BRITT: Because Sam is a traitor, Chris.

SAM: Everything is jumbled now!

BRITT: *(To* SAM*)* That's what you get for siding with a pack of the chemically malformed.

SAM: Be quiet.

BRITT: Speaking of malformity, it seems your own malformations were as false as your loyalty.

SAM: I had you fooled all these years.

BRITT: Tell me—when did those tight-shirts outside the gate get to you? What did they promise you for my head?

SAM: Tight shirts? Please. I work for Francis.

BRITT: *Francis.* Of course. I should have known.

SAM: And so now do all of your malformed persons. They're all on Francis' payroll. They've become Francis' riotous troops. The world will be happy to wipe this terrible manufacturing facility right from its face and let it be replaced by Francis' own nearly exactly the same manufacturing facility. Francis' company will be the cock of the walk.

BRITT: You tell your new boss Francis that a mistake has been made. Francis sent Chris here on what he thought was a "fool's errand of distraction" and instead Francis has handed me a product that will revolutionize every aspect of modern living.

SAM: Sure, sure.

BRITT: Oh yes. It's true.

SAM: And what is the name of this product that will "revolutionize every aspect of modern living".

(A pause)

CHRIS: Um. "Megacosm."

SAM: Megacosm?

CHRIS: Right. Megacosm. "Zindagi."

SAM: "Zindagi?"

BRITT: "Zindagi."

SAM: What is "Zindagi?"

CHRIS: My product.

(SAM points the missile launcher at CHRIS.)

SAM: Put Megacosm on the table.

BRITT: Stay where you are, Chris.

SAM: Put Megacosm on the table or be exploded!

BRITT: If you explode us, then you'll also explode Megacosm and you'll never see what wonder Megacosm brings. And neither will Francis. And neither will the world. So put the missile launcher—it is a missile launcher, isn't it?

SAM: A canon, I call it.

BRITT: Put the *missile launcher* down and we'll all discuss how to work this out without anyone or anything being "exploded." Let's discuss this embroglian. The fate of the world's future is in our hands.

SAM: But Francis—

BRITT: Forget Francis! Francis is a turncoat, a thief and a modern dilicaper! A terrible, honest to god dilicaper from way back years ago. I wouldn't trust Francis with a coat hanger let alone corporate embroglians!

CHRIS: Perhaps you'd like a demonstration.

SAM: A demonstration?

CHRIS: An evaluative demonstration of Megacosm. Yes. Before you decide to explode us.

SAM: A "product demo". Hm. I doubt it will change a single thing. But please. If you feel you must, then go ahead.

(CHRIS *picks up the box and removes the "dolls".* CHRIS *puts the dolls on the table and refocuses the camera. The "dolls" begin to move about as humans, shifting and shaking.* SAM's *eyes go wide as he freezes with wonder as a stupefied* CAROL *looks on.*)

BRITT: The sensation is immediate isn't it?

SAM: Watch those little beings move as they do.

BRITT: "Zindagi."

SAM: It's amazing.

BRITT: Life. "Zindagi."

SAM: Shit my pants. Life.

CHRIS: Megacosm.

BRITT: Megacosm.

SAM: Megacosm.

CAROL: Megacosm.

(*A beat.* BRITT *quickly covers the dolls with the box.*)

(SAM *pulls out a cell phone and makes a call.*)

SAM: Hello… Yes…Francis…no, the riot came
early, one of the malformed…no, the missile didn't
explode… *(Long pause)* Yes. A product. "Megacosm"
they're calling it. "Zindagi."…. I've seen it myself…
Incredible. Yes. Yes. Yes. Yes. Yes. Yes. All right.
(Crosses to the window. Waves) Here I am—Francis, do
you see me? Hello…Hello… Hello… *(Pause)* Okay. I
will. Okay. *(Goodbye)* Ya, shooon-huaaway-tow-gin
(Yeah, all right. See you later. Hangs up the phone.)

SAM: Okay. Francis would like to either blow you up or
to negotiate.

CHRIS: We choose negotiate.

BRITT: I second.

SAM: Negotiate it is.

CHRIS: Great. Then. I would suggest we take the
negotiation to another room that doesn't have a missile
imbedded in the wall.

BRITT: I do all my negotiations here, I'm sorry.

CHRIS: There's a missile imbedded in the wall.

SAM: If the missile were going to explode, it would
have exploded by now.

CHRIS: But—

SAM: This room *is* the negotiation room, Britt is right.

BRITT: Let's sit at the table and stop worrying about
such ridiculous things as missiles.

SAM: I agree, by all means.

BRITT: We can discuss all of this like human beings.

SAM: I'm putting my cannon down.

CHRIS: Please, if you'd both listen—

BRITT: Wait, hold on a moment—

(BRITT crosses to a cabinet and removes a roll of duct tape.)

BRITT: One moment.

(BRITT *crosses to* CAROL. *Grabbing* CAROL, BRITT *duct tapes* CAROL'*s hands together.*)

SAM: *(To* CAROL*)* Sorry. You understand. It's business. We'll be through in a moment.

(SAM *puts duct tape over* CAROL'*s mouth.* BRITT *then pushes* CAROL *into a chair in the corner of the room.*)

(BRITT *and* SAM *sit at the large table.*)

BRITT: Chris? *Chris?* If you please? *(Beat)* If you please?

(A pause. CHRIS *reluctantly sits at the large table.)*

BRITT: Shall I open the negotiation? In this case, Sam, you would be considered Francis' advocate—

SAM: I have been previously approved for advocacy.

BRITT: Good. So. Call to order—

SAM: Order called.

BRITT: I'll begin. *(Beat)* Sam. I've known you my entire life. I've trusted you but now it's been revealed you work for Francis. But this isn't about that. This is about us coming to a natural agreement regarding Megacosm and the future of its global presentation in order to prevent us and the product from being exploded. Chris and I have already secured an agreement—

SAM: An agreement in writing?

BRITT: Yes, bound in writing—

CHRIS: Not bound in writing as of yet.

SAM: Not as of yet?

BRITT: A handshake, bound by a handshake—

SAM: That is not a secure agreement—

BRITT: From corporate case fourteen-oh-nine, yes, a human handshake is a secure agreement—

SAM: Corporate case thrity-seven-six overturned the human handshake as secure agreement.

BRITT: Of course.

SAM: So the agreement is pending contract.

BRITT: Perhaps.

SAM: You'll find I'm more than just an advocate for Francis. I am Francis' mind. I am Francis' matter.

BRITT: Then understand—

(SAM *stands.*)

SAM: No, you understand! *(Takes* BRITT *by the collar)* If this situation were without Megacosm, I would take Megacosm and leave you in chunks on the floor. But I am sincere in my willingness to accept corporate strictures. I will negotiate and I will understand the intricacies.

BRITT: Perhaps we should talk endgame.

SAM: I am willing to move to endgame.

BRITT: Then. *Endgame:*

(CAROL, *turned away, somehow squirms and escapes from the duct tape.)*

SAM: Conjoined profit split?

BRITT: Manufacturing and development at two years, costs covering both with overruns included in the final version.

SAM: Full on, including eastern markets and global facility procurement?

BRITT: Global, yes, but maybe we could squeeze the time—Chris?

CHRIS: —Yes?

BRITT: M & D, less than two or could you do it in one, maybe less? Depending on the number of units manufactured and material costs—how pure do you need the tissue?

CHRIS: Purity is very necessary—

BRITT: So purity can fluctuate, so I'm thinking if we push it, maybe M & D chalks up to eight months at the top.

SAM: It's difficult for me to decide M & D without knowing the properties. *(To* CHRIS*)* Do you have a price quote on generics ?

CHRIS: Generics?

SAM: Harvested tissue. Generics. Have you quotes?

BRITT: I was thinking we've got fundamental tissue supplies of our own that could cut down costs, we would just need some practical harvesters.

CHRIS: What tissue supplies?

SAM: Ah. The malformed. Good thinking. A good crop to draw from.

BRITT: And what of Francis using my malformed child-people as "riotous troops?"

SAM: Recent circumstances require an obvious change in tack.

BRITT: Then we would only need to purchase the harvesters and hire some trained shunters to put them in line, then the process should just be about stripping the flesh. Chris will be on it. Is that comfortable with you, Chris? Taking the lead on developing our systems of in house tissue farming of the child-like malformed, not to mention cranial fluid drainage, electrostasis gathering using nerve-wiring to the interior spinal cord, gelatic aortic blood siphoning—there are probably over a hundred elements we could draw—

CHRIS: I'm unsure if all of those elements are necessary—

BRITT: We've over one thousand malformed persons to extract components from, so better be safe than sorry.

SAM: This all sounds like a healthy, continual plan. I like it.

CHRIS: I don't like it. I don't like it at all.

BRITT: Then where do you suggest we acquire the melded tissue, grafted bone, the hydroxoplasma—

CHRIS: Stripping the flesh from these children—

BRITT: They aren't children and besides, your acquisition of your components for your prototype, how was that completed?

CHRIS: What are you implying?

BRITT: Your underground-market connections.

CHRIS: I used no underground-market connections for my components. I was given my components. Freely.

BRITT: You were? By whom?

CHRIS: My...*mother*. My mother gave me what I needed.

BRITT: Oh.

CHRIS: I'm not ashamed. My mother gave me the majority of her right breast. And a third of a rib beneath. And a liter of her hydroxoplasma.

BRITT: Your parent gave of that to you. Your parent gave it freely.

CHRIS: My mother was sick—

BRITT: And yet you took it from your parent. Freely.

CHRIS: It wasn't the same—

BRITT: It wasn't the same?

SAM: Damnit. Your parent. That takes guts.

CHRIS: My mother gave those components to me freely.

(BRITT *stares at* CHRIS. *A pause*)

BRITT: *(To* SAM*)* I think we can move on, yes?

SAM: I would agree.

BRITT: So, forty percent?

SAM: *(Quickly)* Forty-three—

BRITT: *(Quickly)* Forty-one—

SAM: *(Quickly)* Forty-two—

BRITT: *(Quickly)* And forty-two.

SAM: Agreed. Forty two.

BRITT: Perhaps you'd like to signal Francis we've come to some early understanding regarding in-house product component creation?

SAM: Good idea. I will stand and signal Francis with a proud thumbs up.

(SAM *crosses toward the window. Leaning out,* SAM *waves a hand, giving a signal. Quickly,* BRITT *grabs the knife and stabs* SAM *in the back.* SAM, *jarred, reacts with gurgles.* BRITT *pushes* SAM *out the window and* SAM *falls and dies.*)

CHRIS: Why did you do that?!

(CHRIS *looks out the window, then turns back.*)

CHRIS: You killed Sam!

BRITT: Sam tried to kill us, or did you forget? With the missile, yes?

CHRIS: You stabbed Sam in the back!

BRITT: Not how I would have normally saved an important deal, literally "stabbing someone in the back". But this is Megacosm. It's far too important. And we can not share Megacosm with Francis. Or anyone. Megacosm is our gift to a weary world.

CHRIS: I'm—

BRITT: You're?

CHRIS: I'm—

BRITT: You're angry? Sad? Bothered? Irritated? Frightened? Disgusted? You? You took the right breast, rib bone and a *liter of hydroxoplasma* from your own dillapidating parent. We've done things. We've all done things. None of it should be judged. None can be judged when the meat of the planets has shifted. When you shift the meat of the planets then things tip and miss and when things tip and miss, someone, Chris, someone *needs to be there to catch the cherryfruit*. And those people will be us, Chris. Those people will be us. Me.

(Suddenly, CAROL lunges at BRITT. BRITT, laughing and struggling, pushes CAROL away. After a few moments of struggle, BRITT realizes CAROL has duct taped the missile to BRITT's back.)

BRITT: What the hell is this?

CHRIS: The missile's taped to your back.

BRITT: How? Wait, how did this—Chris? Get this missile off my back. Find the knife.

CHRIS: You pushed the knife out the window.

BRITT: What?

CHRIS: With Sam's back, the knife went out the window.

BRITT: Then yank the missile off.

CHRIS: It might explode.

BRITT: The missile will not explode!

CHRIS: But what if it does and we explode with it? Then, as you stated to Sam, Megacosm will also explode. That's not what you want, is it?

BRITT: No. It isn't.

(The missile begins to hiss.)

BRITT: That's the missile hissing, isn't it?

CHRIS: Yes.

BRITT: We've a handshake agreement, Chris. You are bound to this company. You are bound to it. I'm going downstairs and getting a scissors and cutting this missile from my back but if anything happens remember, you are bound to a human handshake agreement. When I return, we'll go to the lab, dismember your prototype and begin formulative plans for harvesting the malformed of their vital tissue— *(Pointing at* CAROL*)* beginning with that little creep—and thus we'll begin the production process for Megacosm. *(Walks toward the door)* I will return and all will be well.

*(*BRITT *exits the office.* CHRIS *quickly rushes to the office door and slams it shut, locking it behind* BRITT*.* BRITT *looks at* CHRIS *through a window on the door.)*

BRITT: What are you doing!

CHRIS: Locking you out!

BRITT: What?

CHRIS: Your keys went down the duct, or don't you recall! So you've no way back in through this very secure lock and very secure door!

BRITT: Why are you locking me out?!

CHRIS: You're a corrupt, terrible demon! There's no way I will ever go into business with you!

BRITT: Is this about your parent?

CHRIS: This is about the future!

BRITT: Look, I don't care that you harvested pure life force from your parent, okay?

CHRIS: I didn't harvest my parent's pure life force! She offered it to me! To help me with Megacosm!

BRITT: Open the door.

CHRIS: No!

BRITT: We have a deal!

CHRIS: There is no deal.

BRITT: You can't back out of our agreement! WE HAVE A DEAL!

CHRIS: I can back out.

BRITT: We shook hands!

CHRIS: I take it back.

BRITT: No one defies the human handshake! NO MATTER THE LAW! NO MATTER THE PERSON! Do you understand! No one defies the *human handshake!* *(Beat)* You little markitosh. You weak little podilcap. You don't have what it takes. Not in the least. Mark my words—I'll be harvesting *your* parts for Megacosm before the day is out. Mark my vertinating *words!* I'll be harvesting—

(The missile on BRITT's back suddenly explodes, causing a large sound and rafters to fall. CHRIS, grabbing the prototype, and CAROL dive under the large table.)

(A long pause)

CHRIS: Britt exploded.

(CAROL climbs out from under the table.)

CAROL: Chris.

CHRIS: *(To CAROL)* Britt exploded.

CAROL: Chris Yaelenclaven, listen to me.

(A pause)

CHRIS: Wait a minute—

CAROL: We haven't much time.

CHRIS: What happened to your malformed-person, child-like speech patterns?

CAROL: Get out from under the table—

CHRIS: You tell me who you are and what's going on!

CAROL: Get out and I'll explain.

CHRIS: I am not a pawn!

(A pause. CHRIS climbs from under the table.)

CHRIS: All right. Please explain.

CAROL: We've actually met before, you and I.

CHRIS: We have?

CAROL: Many times, in fact. Imagine a voice over a hedge. The voice of a neighbor. The voice of a friend.

(A beat)

CHRIS: *Francis?*

CAROL: Yes.

CHRIS: My neighbor Francis? My friend Francis?

CAROL: Yes.

CHRIS: But if you're Francis—

CAROL: Sam was speaking to one of my operatives before, not me.

CHRIS: But—

CAROL: Five months ago I had my entire body surgically altered so as to match the malformed adult-child laborers who are held prisoner within this facility. My plan was to destroy Britt's corporation from the inside out by breeding chaos, corruption and ultimately a riot that would eventually tear Britt's company to the ground. I sent you here on an errand of distraction on the very day I had planned for my

uprising, not knowing that you, Chris, would do far
more damage than I could have ever dreamed.

CHRIS: But you're the one who manipulated Sam,
you're the one who brought the knife in the room,
you're the one who taped a missile to Britt and blew
Britt up—

CAROL: True.

CHRIS: Then how could you say I've done more
damage than you?

CAROL: *Megacosm*. It is the product demonstration that
has unhinged this corporation and will eventually
unhinge all that this polluted world holds dear.
Everyone will feel its affect—the adult-child slaves, the
wage-devalued, the train-riders, the gutteralls in their
castles. The world's population will be lifted up and
twirled into sublime insanity by you. By Megacosm.

CHRIS: None of that is the purpose of Megacosm.

CAROL: It is. It is Megacosm's *greatest* purpose. To
bring chaos. The cleansing foam of *chaos*. Because when
all persons become gods, then none will be governed.
All will wish to rule. Then all, frustrated, will declare
war on each other. This war will last thousands and
thousands of years. It will be delicious.

CHRIS: Megacosm wasn't created to bring war to this
world. It was created to bring humanity into the realm
of benevolence!

(CAROL *grabs* CHRIS *by the collar.*)

CAROL: That will never happen.

CHRIS: With Megacosm—

CAROL: *(fervent)* You're a starry-eyed flaxengomen.

CHRIS: No. I'm an *absolute realist*.

(*Sirens suddenly sound outside the window.*)

CHRIS: Francis—

(CAROL *lets go of* CHRIS.)

CAROL: The tight-shirts will soon set fire to the building. In order to keep Megacosm safe, we need to leave right now.

CHRIS: But—

CAROL: Chaos is nature, nature is chaos. Chris, you know it's true—

CHRIS: But—

CAROL: It's time to return humanity to nature. It's time for the dawn of a new age.

(*Explosions sound outside the building.*)

CHRIS: Please, Francis. There must be another way.

CAROL: Take my hand.

(CAROL *holds out a hand to* CHRIS. *A pause.* CHRIS *takes* CAROL*'s hand. An explosion.* CAROL *lets go of* CHRIS*'s hand and moves toward the vent.*)

CAROL: We have to hurry—

CHRIS: If you go first, I promise I'll follow.

CAROL: You promise you'll follow?

CHRIS: Yes. If you go first. I'll be right behind you. And I'll do what you say. Because you're right, Francis. I am starry-eyed. But I'm also no fool.

CAROL: Good. I'm glad to hear it.

(CAROL *climbs into the duct and pulls up some slack on the rope for* CHRIS.)

CHRIS: I need to get Megacosm.

(CHRIS *moves toward the box containing Megacosm.*)

CAROL: The explosions are sounding nearer—quickly—

(CHRIS *takes a few steps toward* CAROL.)

CHRIS: I'm sorry. Neighbor. I fundamentally disagree with your terribly flawed and horribly dangerous hypothesis regarding nature and chaos and destruction and deliciousness. And because you've backed me into a corner, I say—

(CHRIS *kicks* CAROL *in the face then pulls on the rope.*)

CHRIS: *(Goodbye)* Tee-em-po-para-Ab-ga-laufin, Pee-yen! *(Time to die, asshole!)*

(CAROL*'s grip loosens on the rope and* CAROL *falls fifteen floors.*)

CAROL: *(Falling, in duct)* Ahhhhhhhhhhhhhhhhh——!!!

(CAROL *lands with a soft, sick thump.*)

(An explosion sounds outside. More sirens sound.)

CHRIS: Oh god.

(CHRIS *rushes to the table and lifts up the box. The "dolls", seen on the monitor, are freaking out.*)

CHRIS: Shh. Shh. Listen. Listen to my words.

(The "dolls" turn toward CHRIS *and listen.)*

CHRIS: It's all over. It's all over. It only seems like bad things are happening, the noise and the confusion. But nothing really bad is happening. I've got you. My friends. My children. I'm protecting you. I've led you into the wilderness. I apologize. But we've come through the other side. And I won't let this happen again. I'll keep you safe. That's a promise I make as your creator.

(The explosions rise as shouts fill the air.)

CHRIS: The world outside may be collapsing, but you'll never be alone. I am here. I will be your true guardian for the rest of time. From my mouth to your ears, you shall be protected!

(More explosions sound.)

CHRIS: What are you saying? I can't hear you! No matter! I understand, there is no need to speak, there is no need—

(The explosions grow louder.)

CHRIS: NOTHING SHALL TEAR US ASUNDER! THE PURITY OF OUR CONNECTION WILL LAST THROUGHOUT TIME! YOUR CHEMICALLY SOUND FORMS WILL EXIST FOR ETERNITY WITHOUT CORRUPTION! ALL WILL BE WELL! ALL WILL BE—

(A large explosion echoes in the room as the lights flicker and a heavy beam from the ceiling smashes into CHRIS, *knocking* CHRIS *to the floor behind the table.)*

(A pause)

*(*CHRIS, *barely illuminated, attempts to stand.* CHRIS's *face is a bloody mass of skull and brain.)*

CHRIS: I can not die. You are my creation. I can not die. I will not die. I can not die.

(A pause. CHRIS *dies. Silence. The glow of the television illuminates the now dimming room.)*

(The "dolls", stand frightened and scared. After a few moments, they group together to silently discuss their plight. They then begin to make their way past the frame of the shining monitor and into a new, dangerous and miraculous world.)

(Blackout)

END OF PLAY